*A Taste of
Chicken Soup for the*

Cat Lover's
Soul®

*Stories of Feline Affection, Mystery
and Charm*

Jack Canfield, Mark Victor Hansen,
Marty Becker, D.V.M., Carol Kline,
Amy D. Shojai

Chicken Soup for the Soul Publishing, LLC
Cos Cob, CT

A Taste of Chicken Soup for the Cat Lover's Soul®
Stories of Feline Affection, Mystery and Charm
Jack Canfield, Mark Victor Hansen, Marty Becker, Carol Kline,
Amy D. Shojai

Published by Chicken Soup for the Soul Publishing, LLC
www.chickensoup.com

Library of Congress Control Number: 2013943999

A Taste of ISBN: 978-1-61159-861-2

Full Book ISBN: 978-1-623610-36-4

Contents

Laser, the Therapist

The moment he reached his little paw through the cage bars at the humane society, I was a goner. I wasn't looking for another cat—I already had two—but was just stopping by to give the animals some attention. When the shelter volunteer, apparently knowing a sucker when she saw one, asked if I would like to hold him, there was no longer any doubt. He came home with me that day.

He was a gorgeous cat, a five-month-old blue-point Siamese with eyes like blue laser beams: thus, his name. Right from the beginning, it was obvious that Laser was an exceptional cat. He loved everyone—the other cats, visitors to the house, even the dog who later joined the household.

I first heard about animal-assisted therapy several months after we adopted Laser. While most of what I heard was about dogs, it occurred to me that Laser would be perfect for this type of work. I signed up for the training class, and, after completing the preliminary requirements, Laser and I passed the test to become registered Delta Society Pet Partners.

While he had always been a little lovebug at home, Laser found his true calling when we began to go on visits. Whether it was with sick kids at the children's hospital, seniors with Alzheimer's disease, or teens in a psychiatric unit, Laser always knew just what to do. He curled up on laps or beside bed-bound patients and happily snuggled close. He never tried to get up until I moved him to the next person. People often commented that they'd never seen a cat so calm and friendly. Even people who didn't like cats liked him!

One young man, who had been badly

burned in a fire, smiled for the first time since his accident when Laser nestled under his lap blanket. A little boy, tired and lethargic from terminal leukemia, rallied to smile, hug Laser and kiss his head, and then talked endlessly about Laser after the visits. Several geriatric patients with dementia, who were agitated and uncommunicative prior to Laser's appearance, calmed down and became talkative with each other and the staff after a visit from my therapeutic feline partner. It has been our hospice visits, though, that I consider the most challenging and rewarding of all our Pet Partner experiences.

One day, I got a phone call telling me about a hospice patient at a nearby nursing home who had requested a visit by a cat. At the time, only one cat—Laser—actively participated in the local program. Even so, my first inclination was to make some excuse not to do it. I have always had issues with death and dying, and a hard time talking about it to anyone, but I quickly realized how selfish I was being—the poor woman was dying, and all she asked was that I bring my cat to visit. I said yes.

A few days later, we made our first visit. Mrs. P. was ninety-one years old, and although her body was weak, her mind was still very sharp. It was a little awkward at first (what do you say to a perfect stranger who knows she's dying?), but Laser was a great conversation catalyst. He crawled into bed with her and curled up right next to her hip—exactly where her hand could rest on his back. She told me stories about the cat she and her husband had years ago.

"See you next week," she said as we got up to leave.

We visited every Sunday during the three months that followed, and a real friendship developed between us. Mrs. P. would excitedly exclaim, "Laser!" every time we appeared at her door and "See you next week!" every time we left. She had been gradually getting weaker, but, one week when we arrived to see her, I was distressed to see that her condition had deteriorated significantly. Still, she smiled and said, "Laser!" when we walked into the room.

She complained of being cold, even though the room was warm, and when Laser cuddled up close to her, she said, "Oh, he's so warm— it feels so good." We had a nice visit, even though Mrs. P. wasn't feeling very well. Her hand never left Laser's back. As we left, she said her usual, "See you next week," and I hoped that was true.

The next Saturday, a phone call informed me that Mrs. P. was going downhill rapidly, and that she probably wouldn't live more than another few days. I asked if we should still come for our visit, and the nurse told me that she thought that would be wonderful.

When we arrived, it was obvious that Mrs. P. was dying. She was fading in and out of consciousness, but when she noticed that Laser and I were beside her bed, she smiled and whispered, "Laser."

She was having a very hard time breathing,

so I told her not to try to talk; we would just sit quietly and keep her company. Laser took his spot on the bed next to her hip, and Mrs. P. rested her hand on his soft back. Neither of them moved from that position for the entire length of our visit. This time, when we got up to leave, Mrs. P. whispered, "Thank you." She knew that there would be no "next week" for us.

A couple of days later, I got the phone call telling me that Mrs. P. had died. I was sad—our weekly visits had been so wonderful—but I was glad that she was no longer in pain. I remembered how I had considered declining to make the hospice visits and was so grateful that I had not.

In our seventh year as a Pet Partner team, Laser and I still make visits to several facilities. Laser, the little cat that nobody wanted, is as beautiful on the inside as he is on the outside, and he continues to brighten the lives of everyone he meets.

~Nancy Kucik

Ringo, the Hero Cat

We adopted our red tabby Manx, Ringo, from a litter of kittens found in a shed outside my mother's nursing home. His mother, who had half a tail, was feral. We fell in love with Ringo when he was only ten days old. He had brilliant red fur, a tiny stump of a tail, bright-blue eyes and a high-pitched, squeaky mew. How could we resist? At the time, we already had three cats and had made up our minds not to get another.

Had we stuck to our promise, we would not be alive today.

Ringo was special from the beginning. He had a wonderful personality and loved nearly everyone who came to visit. An expressive cat, he could move his little bunny puff of a tail in any direction he wanted, depending on how he felt. That red pom-pom tail could speak a thousand words. He was a delight to live with—and, as we were about to discover, a hero, to boot.

Throughout the late spring and summer of 1995, my husband Ray and I developed troubling symptoms, including dizziness, headaches, high blood pressure and oversleeping. Ray was recovering from heart surgery, and I was laid up with a cast on my leg. Naturally, we thought these symptoms were part of our illnesses. We were wrong.

One hot August afternoon, we had the air conditioning going full blast, and the doors and windows shut tight. Ringo, who was inside with us, started slamming his body against the front door of our house and wouldn't stop. In addition, he meowed loudly, over and over. I had never seen him act this way before. Finally, I hobbled over and let him out.

Once outside, he continued his loud

meowing, acting as though he wanted to come back in. Again, I had never seen him act this way. His unusual behavior let me know that I was to follow him. I thought he was going to take me to one of his favorite spots; instead, he led me to the south side of our house, a place on our property that we don't visit too often. Only our air conditioner and gas and water meters are there, hidden behind large bushes. Ringo began to dig in the jagged lava-rock landscaping, about three feet in front of the gas meter. Normally, a cat wouldn't dig among these sharp stones as the edges could easily hurt a paw. Then he lifted his head, opened his mouth and wrinkled his nose to let me know that something smelled awful. When I leaned down next to Ringo, the smell of natural gas nearly bowled me over.

I called the gas company immediately. They sent out an emergency crew, who told us that we were at explosive levels around our foundation. A pilot light or a spark outdoors was all that stood between us and oblivion. In addition, the gas had permeated the walls of our home and traveled up into our bedroom. Our doctor said that if we escaped being killed by a deadly explosion, we would still have succumbed to methane poisoning.

When the plumbers came, they found the leak about three feet in front of the gas meter— right where Ringo had dug. An old steel coupler had split open, and the crack was growing larger as a result of rust and corrosion. Ringo had smelled the escaping gas four feet beneath our landscaping. He led us to the gas leak that we couldn't smell— and the meter didn't register. What a nose for trouble!

After we aired out the house, our health improved rapidly. For his outstanding heroism, Ringo received the American Humane Association's Stillman Award. Only ten cats in nearly a hundred years have received this honor. While many pets have saved their families by insisting that they leave a hazardous situation—saving the pet's own life in the process—it is highly unusual for any animal to lead his family outdoors to alert them to the source of a lethal problem. Ringo, our guardian angel, is gone now, but his extraordinary love and heroic actions will remain with us always.

~Carol Steiner

Time with Marky

When I turned six, my dad bundled my family into the station wagon and drove us to a farm out in the country. By the time we finally rumbled up the dirt road that led to the barnyard, two hours of road ruts and winding turns had reduced my stomach to sheer nerves. Whenever the car jostled from side to side, my stomach lurched precariously as waves of nausea rolled over me.

The station wagon crested the last hill and rolled to a gentle stop. My sister and brother, Susan and Austin, a tangle of limbs fighting for the door, tumbled out and scrambled to the edge of a corral bordered by a weathered fence marked by fading chips of gray paint. Mr.

White, the owner, was already leaning against the fence. A telltale din of yips and yaps punctuated by an occasional yelp rose up and captured our attention like an unexpected eruption of fireworks against a night sky. I followed slowly behind, still nursing my overwrought stomach.

The sight of several puppies frolicking in a patch of stamped grass lifted my spirits. Austin and Susan jumped up and down, pointing at each puppy in turn.

"That one!" shouted Austin. "The one with the white fur and black spots on his tail. I'll name him Spots!"

"*Noooooo,*" whined Susan. "I like the brown one over there in the corner. He's got golden highlights on his ears. We could name him Sunny!"

"I've changed my mind," continued Austin. "I like that gray one. He has ears longer than my hands. And look how furry they are!"

I stood as still as a statue, afraid that the energy generated by the dogs and my siblings would be the undoing of my queasy stomach.

Then, I saw Marky. He appeared as a streak out of the corner of my eye. In a split second, I realized that streak was a cat—a *cat!* He had wavy gray fur and faint black rings on his tail and around his eyes. He separated from the circle of puppies and darted to the edge of the corral, right where we stood. His eyes found mine. I looked back at him with a mixture of surprise and delight. But he wasn't the only one looking at me. Austin and Susan ceased their clamoring and studied us.

"This one here's Marky," said Mr. White. "He's not a dog, as you can see, but no one's bothered to tell him that. He's the life of the bunch, friendly as heck!"

I looked down at Marky again. His eyes, soulful and direct, held a question. I must have answered that question to his satisfaction because, a moment later, he swept his tail back and forth across the dusty ground. He was wagging his tail!

"He must like you," pronounced Mr. White

with a chuckle. "He usually doesn't wag at strangers."

"Dad," I whispered, tugging at his sleeve, "I think he's the one for us. Just look at him." As if understanding my words, Marky turned his eyes toward my dad and gave him the same look he'd just given me.

We settled with Mr. White right then and there.

Marky had never been in a car. In the back of the wagon, he slid back and forth, expressing his excitement over the passing scenery. He got himself too excited, though, because after a short mew, Marky threw up. He whimpered, then fell silent. I scrambled to the back seat and gathered Marky into my arms. We drove all the way home that way, his head cradled in my lap.

In his new home, Marky soon became friends with just about anything that moved. His outgoing ways won over the entire neighborhood. Joey, my next-door neighbor's dog, whether duped by Marky's canine act or merely accepting of Marky's peculiarities, arrived by our sliding door every evening after dinner to call Marky out to play. Marky was only too happy to oblige.

But, when everyone was busy taking care of other business in their lives, Marky liked to plop down in one corner of our porch under a row of wooden benches. He sat there for hours, staring up into the pale-blue sky and out at the empty backyard. As soon as I stepped onto the porch and beckoned him, however, he'd scoot his hind legs out from underneath the bench and scramble eagerly over to me. We spent hours together roaming the woods behind the house. It really didn't matter what we did. Marky always had the time to play whenever I came looking for him.

Then, one day, Marky did not come home from one of his routine jaunts with Joey.

I went to school the next morning, hoping when I got home that I would find Marky biding his time in the corner of the porch. But he didn't appear, and a slow burning behind my eyes intensified. Crushed, I didn't tell anyone at school about Marky's disappearance. On the third day of his disappearance, a rumor began to circulate the school hallways that a dead cat lay by the creek bordering the school's soccer field. My thoughts weighed down with dread all day. As soon as school let out, too scared to go on my own, I ran home and told my parents the rumor. My dad, stern and quiet, flinched at the news and left the house. It was then that my heart emptied.

They found Marky by the creek. The vet told us that he was likely poisoned. The police told us there wasn't anything they could do to catch the culprit.

Several days after our discovery, I sat alone and forlorn in the corner of the porch where Marky once waited for me. I sat there remembering the happiness he had brought into my life. All the tears I had kept to myself coursed down my cheeks, and my body shook in small eruptions. After some time, I felt a presence by my side. I looked up, and, there, sitting next to me, looking up into the pale-blue sky, was Joey. I didn't move an inch. I didn't say one word. Joey looked over at me briefly, then turned his eyes back toward the sky. And there we sat, marking our times with Marky.

I would carry the memory of Marky for years to come. When my grandpa died, I spent time sitting with my dad in front of the television. When my best friend broke up with her first love, I spent time eating ice cream and watching movies in her dorm room. When my mom was diagnosed with cancer, I spent time at home with her while she lay in bed, suffering the effects of chemotherapy. No words were necessary. I'd learned from Marky that one of the best gifts you can give to the ones you love is simply your time.

~Joanne Liu

Happy Endings

It was a Saturday afternoon. As the shelter's cat-program director, I had just completed an adoption. Now, I stood in the adult-cat room, looking around. The doors of the cat cages—we call them cat condos—were open, yet some cats still lounged on the brightly colored, flannel-covered pads inside them. There were a few cats lying on the wide, sunny window ledge, watching the world outside or just snoozing contentedly. I looked up and saw Otis walking along the catwalk, a network of boards suspended from the ceiling that cats access by climbing a tall, rope-covered column in the corner that doubles as a scratching post. Moo stuck his head through the cat door from the screened-in porch, just to make sure he wasn't missing anything important. Satisfied I wasn't bearing food, he withdrew his furry black-and-white head, and, through the window, I saw him leap gracefully onto one of the chairs on the porch to resume his nap in the dappled sunlight. The scene was one of pleasant, clean, feline serenity.

What a difference a year makes, I thought. A year ago, Noah's Ark Animal Foundation's cats were all in foster care, as well as some cramped temporary housing in my own home. It hadn't been easy, but we'd made it through. It had been just one more stage in our journey—rising from the ashes of the tragedy that had nearly destroyed us seven years before.

In March 1997, local teenage boys broke into our shelter, killing seventeen cats and seriously injuring a dozen more. The story generated headlines across the country— it was even voted *People* magazine's 1997 "Story of the Year," based on the level of reader response. When the young men were found guilty of only misdemeanors, many animal lovers were outraged, feeling the boys had been let off with too light a punishment. Yet even this dark cloud had a silver lining: Using the incident as a banner, we at Noah's Ark, along with other animal-welfare organizations, were able to persuade state legislators to stiffen the animal-cruelty laws in Iowa, and in several other states as well.

But, as an organization, we experienced some tough times. The tragedy had been traumatic for all involved, and it took a while to recover emotionally. Then, five years later, we were forced to move from the facility we had been using for more than ten years. We scrambled and found a temporary home for our shelter dogs on the farm of a generous couple who supported the foundation's work. The cats were scattered in homes throughout the area.

We kept our doors open—rescuing and finding homes for as many dogs and cats as we could, as well as promoting spay/neuter education and activities. In the meantime, we were slowly raising money to buy land to build a new shelter. We were doing the best we could under the circumstances. The strain was enormous, and, privately, I wondered how much longer we could go on that way.

Then a miracle happened—the kind that makes you pinch yourself to be sure you aren't dreaming. A fairy godmother appeared, waved her magic wand, and— *poof!*—*we* had our very own brand-new shelter. Well, not exactly, but close! The administrator of a charitable foundation heard about our work. Our benefactress, who was appropriately named Miss Kitty, made a sizable donation, which— in addition to the money we had already raised— enabled us to build a shelter: the beautiful, modern, designed-for-animals building in which I now stood.

Of course, it took a lot more than a *"poof!"* to build the shelter. A great deal of work went into the research, design and building of our facility, because not only is our shelter clean and comfortable for animals, staff, volunteers and visitors, it is also kind to the Earth. Our building is "green," which means it is energy-efficient and has healthy interior-air quality because it was built with nontoxic construction materials and designed to take advantage of the sun for lighting and thermal power. The cats and dogs at Noah's Ark really seem to like the building. This is important because, even though we hope their stays will be brief, some animals spend a long time with us. Once we take an animal in, it remains with us until we find it a home—no matter how long that takes.

Doing rescue work isn't always fun. There is a high level of frustration because we can't save them all, and also because we worry when an animal doesn't seem to be adjusting well to shelter life or is returned after an unsuccessful adoption. Nevertheless, there are a lot of happy endings—and they are what keep us going.

I smiled, thinking of the adoption I had just completed. Kenny left this afternoon in the arms of a woman who couldn't see him, but loved him all the same. Kimberly, who is blind, immediately fell in love with Kenny, a long-time Noah's Ark resident, who had been passed over repeatedly by other potential adopters, probably because he was considered too ordinary: a black shorthair cat, no longer a kitten.

Of course, Kenny had done his part. Kimberly wanted a cat who would be drawn to her. Just a few moments after she took a seat in the adoption-room rocking chair, Kenny was on her lap, extolling his own virtues in his own way. Sometimes, I can only marvel at how these cat adoptions transpire; so often, it seems that it is the cat or kitten who adopts a human family, not the other way around. In any case, Kenny and Kimberly connected in a way that was beyond mere visual attraction. It was a particularly satisfying happy ending for me because I knew how much Kenny had to give.

Leaving the cat room, I looked around and said, "Don't worry, guys. Soon, it'll be your turn to go home with someone nice." Then I closed the door and walked through the happiest ending of all—Noah's Ark's new building, which houses our reborn spirit and provides shelter for the steady stream of animals who need and receive our care.

~Janet Mullen

The Call of the Lobster

Basil Rathcoon and his half-sister Agatha Coonstie were the first Maine Coon cats that I had ever had, and I quickly became accustomed to their trilling, musical sounds, which my husband and I refer to as "talking." Basil, a twenty-pound male, is, by far, the more vocal of the two; as a kitten, he developed a particular language for talking to his favorite plaything, a stuffed toy lobster.

The "call of the lobster" always occurred when Basil, carefully clutching the red toy in his jaws, moved his little friend. Every day, the lobster was taken to breakfast, to naptime in Basil's bed, to watch television on the sofa, to dinner and, finally, to bed. Of course, the lobster, "Mr. Johnny-on-the-Spot," helped with various household chores, such as doing the dishes or the laundry. Basil made sure that he and his friend participated in every activity that involved the family, so, each time Basil moved his lobster, he would pick him up and explain to him—using his entire lung capacity—the next task on their agenda. No matter where I was in the house, I could always hear them coming.

As so often happens in childhood friendships, I feared that the two would grow apart as Basil matured. But the two remained fast friends, even though the poor lobster suffered many tragedies, such as being dropped into the water bowl by Basil's jealous brother Rochester, a longhair red tabby. The lobster had to be washed, dried and refitted with catnip—via a minor surgical procedure—before he was fit to travel again. All seemed well. Until one day, when the toy disappeared, and the call of the lobster ceased.

My husband and I were saddened by the

loss of the musical cries, but what we found even more distressing was the change in Basil's behavior. Although he had always been a fantastic jumper, energetic and a little too intelligent for his own good, he had never destroyed the furniture or broken anything fragile. So when he started stretching his arms through the upstairs banister in order to swipe at the artificial long-stem flowers in an antique vase that had belonged to my deceased mother-in-law, I became upset. I feared that the sometimes-naughty Rochester had taught Basil the art of attacking fake flowers.

For several months, I moved the vase of flowers around the house to different locations. Each time, Basil would try amazing stunts to reach it. One day, disgusted by yet another of Basil's attempts to massacre the flowers, I picked up the vase to move it. My husband, who was standing nearby, said, "Why is there a pair of eyes looking at me?"

Startled, I set the vase down on the dining-room table and backed away. My fearless husband reached into the flowers and pulled out—Basil's lobster.

We sat down on the floor, called Basil to us and reunited him with his wayward friend. Basil sniffed the lobster, then picked up his pal and marched him upstairs to the bedroom and placed him in a circular cat bed. For two days, the lobster remained grounded in the bedroom, but at the end of the lobster's detention, he was allowed to resume his normal traveling duties.

Basil is now five years old. Sadly, the irreplaceable lobster was dunked one too many times in the water-bowl by Rochester, so Basil adopted a red catnip-stuffed mouse, and a new loving friendship has developed.

Even our female tortie, Pyewacket, caterwauls to her favorite friend, a green sparkling glitter ball—though she is not able to make the same musical sounds that Basil can. I am the only person I know whose pets have pets of their own, which makes for a happy, if somewhat loud, family.

~Susan Isaac

Mayor Morris

In his younger days, our cat Morris, now sixteen years old, was the mayor of our neighborhood. A stray I adopted from our local animal shelter when he was about a year old, Morris settled into life as an apartment dweller quite easily, content to give up scavenging for meals and dodging dogs and cars for food from a can and a sunny square of carpet to nap on. Yet as happy as he was to have a home, Morris never completely gave up his love of the outdoors. He would sit for hours by the open bedroom window in our apartment, his nose pressed to the screen, sniffing the air and watching the activity in the park three stories down. At first, I thought he wanted to be out in the fresh air and sunshine, but soon, I realized that it was the hustle and bustle of the outside world that he missed.

When my husband and I moved to our first home—a red-brick row house on a tiny street in Philadelphia— Morris would sit with us on our stoop or lounge in our miniscule front yard greeting the neighbors and holding court. In the spring, he'd sit on our elderly neighbor's stoop, a pace or two from our own door, supervising her attempts to plant flowers in her patch of dirt. On Halloween, he'd wait at the front door for the trick-or-treaters, his amber eyes glinting in the candlelight from the jack-o'-lanterns. And when our daughter started walking, he'd station himself on the sidewalk in front of the house, keeping a watchful eye on her as she clattered past him, up and down the street, behind her push toys. Morris never seemed to want to venture more than a few feet from his own front door.

A few years later, expecting twins and

suddenly needing much more space, we bought a house in a nearby suburb, on a quiet street that wound around in an elongated oval, beginning and ending at the top of the hill. The only traffic was the morning and evening rush of a half-dozen cars taking neighbors to and from work, and the mail and UPS vans making their occasional deliveries.

One midsummer morning, when we had been living there a few months, I walked to the end of our driveway to collect the newspaper, Morris trotting at my heels.

"Is that your cat?" someone called, as I bent to retrieve the papers.

I straightened up. A trim woman in her fifties wearing bright-pink walking shorts and a sleeveless button-down shirt was crossing the lawn toward me. I knew she lived in the house to the right of ours with her husband and a twenty-something-year-old son, but I had not yet met her. I had not met many of our neighbors since I had been closeted in the house for most of the late spring and early summer, first on bed rest, then taking care of my newborns.

"Yes," I said as she stepped onto my driveway. "This is Morris. And I'm Meg. It's nice to finally meet you."

"It's nice to meet you, too," she said, introducing herself and shaking my hand. "And it's nice to know your name," she said, squatting to scratch Morris behind his ears. "My husband will be happy, too," she said, gazing up at me. "Now he'll know what to call him," she said.

My face must have shown my confusion because she laughed.

"My husband and your cat—Morris—have breakfast together on our patio every morning," she explained, standing up. "One morning just after you moved in, my husband went out with his coffee and the newspaper and found Morris sitting in one of the chairs. They had a lovely chat. Now, Morris waits for him on the patio every morning. My husband reads the paper to him, and they discuss world events, don't you Morris?"

Morris had apparently made more friends in the neighborhood than I had in the few months we'd been living there. Every morning he'd meet our neighbor on his back patio for coffee and conversation. Then he'd spend some time playing with the poodles in the house to the left, sitting in the grass at the edge of our driveway just beyond the boundary of their invisible fence, while the dogs ran back and forth, barking and wagging their tails.

When the fall came, he began ambling to the foot of our driveway every afternoon to wait for the school buses to drop the neighborhood kids at the top of the street. He'd greet each kid as they came down the hill past our house, accepting pats and scratches behind his ears. And on Halloween, he took up his place next to the pumpkins and greeted the trick-or-treaters.

Shortly before Thanksgiving every year, our neighbors to the right would travel to Florida, where they spent the winter. Morris took this as a sign to retreat into the house for the winter. In April, when the weather grew warm again, our neighbors would return, and Morris would resume his daily round of social activities. But one spring, our neighbors didn't return. Instead, a for-sale sign appeared in front of the house. Our neighbors had decided to stay in Florida, their son told us when he came by one afternoon to check on the house.

"Oh, by the way," he said, getting into his car, "my dad said to say hi to your cat. He really misses their conversations."

I knew Morris missed those conversations, too. He still waited on the patio every morning for his friend to come out for breakfast.

The house sold quickly, to a Korean family with two teenage daughters and an elderly grandmother. They were friendly neighbors. The girls always stopped to talk to our children when they were playing outside, and the parents would wave and chat for a few minutes whenever we happened to be picking up our newspapers or getting into our cars at the same time. But the elderly grandmother never said a word, ducking her head and looking the other way the few times we'd seen her in the front yard. I'd overheard her granddaughters speaking to her in Korean and suspected that she didn't know any English.

One summer morning, I was watering the plants on our back deck when I heard the soft quavering voice of the elderly grandmother on her patio below. She was speaking quickly and quietly, a steady stream of words in Korean. Occasionally, she'd pause as if asking a question, but I heard no voice answering back. *She must be talking to herself,* I thought. Quietly, I peered over the deck railing. She was sitting at the wrought-iron table with a cup of tea. Morris, in the chair next to her, was listening intently as she talked to him.

The mayor of the neighborhood had done it again! Morris had a new breakfast companion, and our elderly Korean neighbor had a new friend.

~M. L. Charendoff

Coco's Cat

"She looks bored," pronounced my daughter, home for a short visit from college.

We both studied the longhaired gray cat I'd adopted the previous week from the D.C. Humane Society. Ever since I'd brought her home, Coco, who had been the most vivacious cat at the shelter, had been listless and apathetic. I tried changing her food, gave her vitamins, played with her more in the evenings. Nothing seemed to pique her interest.

"Maybe she needs a pet," smirked my know-it-all daughter.

A few nights later, I was startled awake by a long, mournful wail coming from a dark mound on the sill of my open bedroom window. "Coco, for goodness sake, what *is* your problem?" I said as I scooped her up and plopped her in her usual nighttime spot at the end of my bed. As soon as I'd turned off the light, she jumped back down and resumed her wailing position. I won that round by depositing her on the other side of a closed bedroom door, but her scratching kept me awake most of the night.

For the next couple of days, Coco spent most of her time on the windowsill, alternately mewling and wailing—all the while, glaring accusingly at me.

"Let her out," advised my daughter, over the phone from her college dorm.

"Are you serious?" I said. Busy Wisconsin Avenue ran right in front of my apartment building. "She wouldn't last long enough for me to double-lock my door."

After a few more days of listening to an emotionally distressed feline—one who was now on a kitty hunger strike—I was ready to take my daughter's advice. But my second-floor apartment was too high for a cat to come and go. I made a reconnaissance trip to the courtyard in back of my apartment building and looked up at my window, barred for inner-city security. Coco stared down at me in silent appeal.

I widened my gaze. An old, wooden ladder was half- hidden behind some shrubs. I leaned it against the building under my window. There was still a five-foot gap, but it was worth a try.

I tried not to think about other city critters that might find the makeshift entrance inviting as I opened the window just enough for Coco to slip under. She had no trouble jumping down to the top of the ladder. As I watched her disappear around the corner of the building, I prayed she'd be able to make the jump back up again—and that she'd be safe.

I know it's irresponsible to let house cats outside, especially in a busy city, but Coco's need to go out was so intense, I couldn't help but believe she knew what she was doing.

Even so, I probably glanced out that window every quarter hour for the rest of the afternoon.

Just as I was starting to worry, I heard the rattle of the mini-blind covering the open window. Coco jumped down to the floor, then turned to stare back at the window.

Almost immediately, a black-and-white head pushed aside the blind. Coco gave an encouraging meow, and the newcomer jumped down. The cats touched noses as I stared in disbelief.

The visiting cat wasn't very clean—her spots were more gray than white—and she was extremely thin, except for her belly, which showed obvious signs of late-stage pregnancy. I couldn't imagine how Coco had induced her to make that last five-foot jump onto the sill, let alone enter a strange apartment. But there she was, looking around my bedroom while Coco gently licked her neck and back.

"This is not a good idea," I grumbled as I put out a second dish of food and introduced the visitor to the litter box. "Tomorrow, she has to go to the Humane Society. After all, that's the responsible thing to do with stray cats, especially pregnant stray cats." Both cats ignored my comments.

The next morning, I pulled my cat carrier from under my bed and went looking for the stray. She wasn't in any of the rooms of the apartment. Finally, I noticed Coco sneaking into my hall coat closet. When I opened the door, I found the visitor cat stretched out in a box of winter garments nursing four tiny fur balls. Okay, forget the Humane Society. How heartless would I have to be to turn out a new mother and four adorable babies?

Polly, as I now called her, and her babies stayed in the closet for a couple of weeks, until the babies got big enough and brave enough to venture out into the apartment. During that time, it was apparent Polly wasn't exhibiting natural maternal behavior. She didn't even groom herself, let alone her babies. Coco assumed responsibility for cleaning, cuddling and playing with the kittens. Polly merely served as wet nurse, showing no interest in her offspring, as Coco taught them how to wash and defend themselves, and to use the litter box. In fact, Polly showed little interest in anything and spent most of her time staring into space. As soon as the kittens were weaned, I took her to my vet for spaying and shots. In the course of his examination, he discovered Polly was deaf and possibly brain-damaged.

On the other hand, the kittens were as active and curious as kittens everywhere, getting into everything and getting bigger each day. I decided I would keep Polly and started looking for adoptive homes for the kittens. Within a week, I found homes for all four.

The day the last kitten left, Coco retreated under the couch and refused to come out for her evening meal, occasionally emitting soft kitty moans. The next morning, she was still there, and no amount of coaxing could budge her. I thought about taking a sick day from work, but I was afraid that "my cat's depressed because she lost her foster kittens" was not a legitimate excuse for absence. I rushed home after work and, when Coco failed to meet me at the door, looked under the couch. There was only empty space and some shed fur. I made a tour of the apartment and finally found both cats curled up face-to-face in the box of winter clothes in the hall closet, Polly with both paws around Coco's neck. Coco looked up when I opened the door, but Polly just continued licking Coco's face. Both cats were purring loudly.

Coco and Polly still live with me and are never very far away from each other. Coco never eats her food until she's sure Polly is beside her at her own dish, and she faithfully grooms her daily. Polly remains unresponsive to my attention. She seems happiest when cuddled up against Coco.

I guess my daughter was right: Coco did need a pet, someone to take care of. And Polly and her kittens would never have survived for long on their own. How Coco knew this, I'll never know. And, somehow, by some instinct, Polly recognized when Coco was grieving and was able to offer the comfort she needed, comfort that could only come from another cat.

~Sheila Sowder

Elvis Has Left the Building

He had been my best friend and companion for more than twelve years, a first-year anniversary present from my husband when I told him I wanted something soft and warm to take care of. He had been with me through several jobs, earthquakes, fires, the L.A. riots, and five or six moves to different apartments. He was my surrogate child, my baby, my pal and protector when my husband was working late. He took care of me, followed me everywhere and loved me unconditionally.

So, when the veterinary surgeon told me that my beloved cat Elvis would die within a few weeks, I was devastated. I had just become pregnant with my first child, and so badly wanted my baby to know Elvis and come to love him as much as my husband and I did.

It had happened so quickly: One week, my husband and I noticed that our usually healthy and robust black-and-white cat was rapidly losing weight. After a few more days passed, we noticed a distinct loss of energy, and we took Elvis to be examined.

Finding an abnormality in the blood, the vet referred us to a wonderful internal-medicine group for animals. There, Elvis suffered through a battery of tests, which eventually determined his fate. He had a rare form of mast-cell cancer that was untreatable. But that didn't stop him from befriending the receptionists and lab technicians, who quickly grew to love him. Whenever we would come to pick him up, we could hear them in the back yelling, "Elvis has left the building!"

As the weeks went on, the doctor taking care of Elvis left it to us to decide how to proceed. We decided to try anything we could to keep Elvis alive and give him a chance to fight.

That meant spending more than five thousand dollars, and coming in two to three times a week to give Elvis blood transfusions and chemotherapy—none of which guaranteed his recovery. But we had to try.

At night, Elvis slept cuddled up in bed near us. He was so gaunt and weak that he needed our body heat to stay warm, and he would press his head against my arm as if to say, "Stay close." During the days he was home, he would lie on the couch and sleep, occasionally raising his head and giving me his trademark meow, a strange, nasal *"maaaaa!"*

As the baby inside me grew bigger, Elvis grew weaker, and my husband and I realized he was losing his battle with cancer. It was January, and my baby was due in March. If only Elvis could hold on a little longer—but, as the month wore on, it was obvious the chemo was not working. Elvis had lost more than half his body weight, and he could barely move. His blood levels were dangerously anemic. The doctor didn't even think he could handle another transfusion.

So, on a cold day at the end of January, my husband and I carried Elvis back to the doctor's office one final time. In what seemed like a surreal dream, we were led through the surgery area to a room in the back called "the grieving room." It was a peaceful, friendly room with a couch and curtains, designed to make a painful process a little more comfortable. We were given a half hour to say our final good-byes. Then the doctor came in, said a prayer for Elvis, and injected a syringe into a vein.

As I felt my friend, my beloved Elvis, go limp in my arms, I held him close to my huge belly, hoping that maybe part of his spirit would go into my unborn child. It was a silly fantasy, but it kept me going long enough to leave the office without crying—until I heard one of the lab techs say sadly, "Elvis has left the building." The receptionist was crying, and, as she hugged me, I broke down in tears.

It took a few weeks before I could get

through the day without weeping. Reminders of Elvis were everywhere. But, as March approached, my focus turned to my upcoming C-section. Our little boy, Max, was about to make his appearance into the world. My husband and I had picked out his name, Maxwell Gordon Jones, and, on March 19, as scheduled, he was born—big and bouncy and healthy.

During Max's first night in the hospital, he made all kinds of strange baby noises, including a very distinct nasal *"maaaaa!"* My husband and I gasped, staring at each other. Could it be? *"Maaaaa!"* We laughed as we pondered the idea that our child had somehow absorbed Elvis's spirit. And, when Max napped next to me in the bed, I melted when he pressed his head against my arm, as if to say, "Stay close."

When we filled out the birth certificate, we decided to add a little something special to Max's name: Maxwell Gordon Elvis Jones. Now, six months later, Max acts more and more like the feline brother he will never meet—loving, affectionate and cuddly—and this comforts me.

I took Max grocery shopping recently. As I stood in line, holding him in my arms, I noticed a tabloid headline and had to laugh. It read: "Elvis Lives!"

No kidding, I thought, as I squeezed my son and kissed him on the cheek.

~Marie D. Jones

Conversation with a Cat

About eight years ago, my girlfriend Gale and I bought a cabin in Flagstaff, Arizona, to use as a summer getaway. The cabin needed extensive renovation, so, during that first summer, while Gale worked in Tucson, where we lived at the time, I traveled to Flagstaff for a week or so each month to make the necessary repairs.

One warm afternoon, while I was working on the deck, I heard a meow. Looking up, I saw a half-grown cat standing thirty or forty feet away from me near our woodpile. I figured she was one of the feral cats that lived in the area. Studying her for a moment, I meowed back. Encouraged, the cat meowed again. I replied, briefly wondering what we were saying to each other. A few more mews were exchanged before she finally skittered off into the woods.

She obviously enjoyed our conversation because she came back. Every day that week, I saw her running through the yard or sunning herself in a protected spot near the woodpile.

I have always had a soft spot for cats—we had two at home in Tucson—and so I began to leave food out for her. If I was around, she wouldn't go near it, but if I was inside, she'd come and lick the bowl clean. I tried holding food out to her in my hand, but it was still too frightening for her. She needed her space, so I gave her a wide berth.

Something about this particular cat touched me. I wanted to convince her to let me pet her. I could see that a whole person was just too much for her to handle, so while she ate her dinner on the porch, I put some cat food on my fingers, lay down on the floor just inside the door, and stuck my arm and hand with the food on it out the door—in clear view from her food dish. It took a few days of this dinnertime routine, but soon she was licking the food off my fingers with no problem.

Next, I brought her food bowl out to the porch and, instead of leaving, sat near her while she ate. She quickly made the connection that the big, scary human also meant delicious food. She was wary, but her hunger was stronger than her fear.

She was fairly unremarkable in appearance. Her short, smooth coat was white with patches of charcoal gray that was almost black. Her face was mostly white, but she had a dark spot above one eye and around one ear. Her back was all dark gray except for her one unusual marking: a small patch of white, shaped like an arrowhead, in the middle of her spine.

One day as she had her nose buried deep in her bowl, I reached over and ran my hand along her back. She startled, but didn't bolt. I continued to pet her and talk to her while she finished her food.

We had made definite progress, but this was where it stopped. She let me sit near her and pet her during meals. She would even come up on the porch and hang around if I was sitting on a chair reading, but she wouldn't come inside and wouldn't let me pick her up or hold her. We'd hit a wall, and she wouldn't go an inch further.

Still, we had a connection. If I left to run errands, as soon as my car pulled into the drive, my standoffish cat would come running to greet me. I decided to name her Moki, after the Moki Dugway, a spectacular stretch of road that winds through the red rocks and desert of southern Utah. Something about the arrowhead on her back seemed to resonate with that area.

For the next few months, whenever I went back to Tucson, I paid Jessica, a neighbor's daughter, to put out food for Moki while I was gone. Jessica told me that Moki ate her food, but wouldn't let Jessica near her. She reserved that privilege for me. And so our pattern continued: Every time I pulled into the drive that summer and fall, Moki seemed to sense my presence and came running.

Then, one October afternoon, I pulled in, but Moki didn't come. I was uneasy, but not alarmed. Perhaps she was off hunting. A little while later, Jessica's mother knocked on my door. "I have some bad news," she told me.

One evening, my neighbor explained, when Jessica came over to put out food for Moki, somehow the family dog got out of the yard and followed Jessica over to my house. Moki was waiting near the woodpile for her dinner when the dog came up behind her and attacked her. Jessica screamed at him to stop, but the dog shook Moki violently before Jessica could reach them. A moment later, the dog dropped the cat, and Moki took off, bloody and injured. She didn't know where Moki was—or how she was—but she wasn't hopeful about an injured cat's chances in the predator-filled woods around our houses.

I immediately jumped in the car and went

looking along the woods by the road. I called and called, but heard and saw nothing. Moki, if she was alive, was long gone. That visit I spent part of every day searching for Moki. All that I found was some fur by the woodpile, a horrible reminder of what had occurred. Deeply saddened, I left Flagstaff a week later, sure I'd seen the last of Moki.

Winter passed, and I made one or two trips to Flagstaff to work on the cabin. There was never any sign of Moki. I was surprised at the pain I felt at the loss of this cat who had kept such an unbending boundary between us. I put the memory of Moki in a compartment in my heart and tried to forget about her.

When May rolled around again, I made another trip to Flagstaff to put the finishing touches on the cabin where I hoped Gale and I could spend some time together that summer.

Late one afternoon, as I was working inside with the door open to let in the spring breeze, I heard it: a faint meow. I dropped what I was doing and ran outside.

There she was, coming toward me as fast as she could— on three legs. Her fourth leg was still there, but she wouldn't put any weight on it.

I knelt down and petted Moki gently so I wouldn't frighten her, but I was so happy to see her, I found myself picking her up and holding her close to me. She didn't struggle. Instead, she purred loudly as I carried her inside.

I called Gale to share the good news. She thought I should get Moki to a vet as soon as possible. That night, Moki slept with me without ever leaving the bed.

The next morning, I took her to the vet. He X-rayed her leg and said that it had been broken and had knitted badly, but he didn't recommend putting her through the trauma of re-setting it. He felt that, in time, once the leg was fully healed, she would begin using it again. I asked the vet to spay her and give her shots and worming medicines. The following day, when I picked her up at the vet's office,

Moki snuggled in my arms as if she had always done so. The wall between us had disappeared.

Moki and I have remained close. In fact, there haven't been very many occasions over the last eight years when we've been apart; she even travels with us on vacations. I don't know how she survived that snowy winter, alone and injured out in the cold, but I'm glad she did. I don't know which one of us was happier at our reunion; today, I can't tell you which one of us is more attached to the other. Gale says that Moki looks at me with "Nancy Reagan eyes." Moki is clearly my cat, and I am clearly her person. And life is sweeter because of it.

You just never know where a conversation with a cat might lead you.

~Hoyt Tarola

Always Room for One More

One day last spring, we were driving home from a Saturday afternoon's shopping trip. It was four-thirty, peak traffic time on the major four-lane road through town. I was tired and gazing without focus at the shops and houses passing by. My husband Fred, who was driving, suddenly said in an outraged voice, "What was that?"

"What?" I asked, suddenly alert.

He looked to our right and yelled, "It's a kitten!"

He had seen a small, fuzzy ball tossed from the right side window of the car in front of us. Too stunned to take note of the car's license plate, Fred swerved into the first available driveway, put the car in park and ran back to where he'd seen the kitten land by the curb. I sat in the car imagining the worst. What chance would a kitten have in that kind of traffic?

A few minutes later, Fred returned and handed me an eight-week-old white bundle of fur, with orange stripes behind each ear and an orange rump. The kitten was trembling and looked dazed, but did not seem injured. Then I noticed he was missing his tail. *Oh no*, I thought, *he's been run over*. Looking more closely, I saw that he had been born that way.

"He's part Manx," I said. I held him close to me, petting him and talking in soft tones. Turning to Fred, I said, "Now what?"

We already had longtime housemates: two adult cats in their early teens. At Christmas, we had added a young part-Persian stray who had been hanging around the antique mall where Fred worked. It had taken three months for the resident cats and the newcomer, Pooh, to get accustomed to each other. Now we were bringing home another? And to a house not much larger than a two-bedroom apartment, no less.

Fred said, "Let's just take him home and get him calmed down. On Monday, I'll take him to the pet-grooming shop." The woman who ran the shop had a soft heart for stray cats and took them in until she could find homes for them.

We snuck the kitten into the house and put him into one of the small bedrooms, along with food, water, kitty litter and an old towel to sleep on. It didn't take long for the other cats to discover the interloper. One by one, they planted themselves in front of the closed door, demanding silently to know what was going on. Squeek, the dominant older cat, was clearly dismayed and gave me glowering looks every time I walked by the bedroom door. He wanted me to know that there simply was no more room in the house or in his heart to accept another cat. "It's okay, old man," I said, leaning over to stroke his silky head, "we are only keeping him for the weekend."

By Sunday, the kitten had gotten comfortable with his new arrangement and was looking for entertainment. I found myself checking on him frequently, petting him and dangling a string for him to attack. When I picked him up to hold him, he purred intensely and rubbed his nose affectionately on mine.

"Don't get too attached," Fred warned.

"No problem," I said, "I can't manage another cat." Two cats had seemed easy. Two cats to locate. Two cat dishes to wash. Two cats to brush and medicate when needed. Eight paws worth of nails to trim. Two cats who sometimes shared the bed at night. Then the third arrived. Suddenly, my morning routine was overturned. Where was each cat? Who had been fed, and who hadn't? Why was I always running out of clean dishes for them? While the older ones slept, the young one wanted me to come out and play. Life had gotten a lot busier with the addition of just one. I couldn't imagine adding a fourth.

Sunday night, Fred and I reassured one another of our decision not to keep him. "It will be too hard on the older cats," I said.

"They are already stressed by Pooh."

"Yes," he agreed, "and there is the added expense of cat food and vet care." Three cats were quite enough, we concluded.

Monday morning, I said good-bye to the kitten and left for work. As I drove away, I thought about the fact that the tiny face with the huge amber eyes would not be there when I got home. I started to cry. "Stop that," I admonished myself out loud. "You can't take in every stray who comes your way." Still, I could not shake the heaviness from my heart.

I fretted all morning and couldn't focus on my work. I found myself wanting to call Fred and tell him to forget taking the kitten to the pet shop. Each time I reached for the phone, however, the prior night's words of reason stopped me.

That night, I arrived home to find that the kitten was gone, safely ensconced in a cage at the grooming shop, according to Fred. I felt like a traitor. "He trusted us," I said despondently, "and now he sits alone in a cage. How frightened he must be. Who knows if anyone will adopt him or how long it will take." Fred didn't respond and was uncharacteristically quiet all evening.

My mood was no lighter the next morning. I could think of nothing but the kitten. By midafternoon, I had made a decision. I called home and said to Fred, "Go get the kitten. How much work is one more, anyway?"

"No need," Fred replied. "He's right here in my lap. I couldn't stand it, so I went back and got him this morning." He had given the shop owner a donation to help with the other stray cats, thanked her and told her we'd decided to keep him. She had smiled and said, "It doesn't surprise me."

"We are nuts," I said.

"I know," he responded, laughing.

Skeeter is now a happy established member of the family. Yes, there was a period of adjustment for both cats and humans. Squeek still reminds him with an occasional cuff to the head that Squeek is the boss cat and has full ownership of the new cat bed. Pooh, at first cautious, is now delighted to have a playmate to chase around the yard. Shadow, the elder cat, has become the surrogate mother, giving the kitten long loving licks. They often sleep together, Shadow's front paw cuddling the kitten.

Somehow, my routine has adjusted itself— or I've adjusted to it. The cats have their own feeding schedule so that there are never more than two of them in our tiny kitchen at one time. They seem to understand the two- cats-on-the-bed-at-one-time rule and they rotate occupancy. Skeeter has established an evening ritual of racing first to Fred's lap and then to mine to give each of us an affectionate glad-you're-mine buss on the nose.

All new life brings teachings—or reminders—of past lessons lost. In this case, I am reminded that, even when the head says "impossible," the heart can always find room for one more.

~Roberta Lockwood

Panther and the Pigeons

Panther wasn't the kind of cat who would cuddle up in your lap and purr; she was feral. Her name suited her. A beautiful black cat with piercing green eyes, she roamed— and, in her own way, ruled—the neighborhood. Shunning people, she strutted as if she owned the block.

Other cats gave her room. Panther showed no mercy to birds or mice, and didn't run from dogs, either. She had been known to fly out of nowhere at unsuspecting dogs, then take off in a black flash. She had everything under control in her territory—except for Artie's backyard.

In Artie's yard, there was a pigeon coop that stymied her. Panther's pride could not allow this. She eyed the coop up and down, but hadn't been able to enter it. Panther's big obstacle was Artie. He secured the coop with two latches and was always on the lookout, thwarting her plans. Sometimes, he would chase her out of the yard, but he couldn't keep her away. Panther would wait until he was gone, then slink back to circle the coop, again and again. At the first sight of Artie, though, she took off.

One morning, as Artie walked across the yard, Panther darted by in her usual flash of black, then disappeared. Only this time, he saw that she had darted from *inside* the coop, exiting through a small hole in the mesh. Artie was afraid to look. How many birds had she killed or maimed? Cursing the cat, he slowly looked inside the coop.

The birds were all there, alive and unhurt. They weren't even in the state of frenzy he had expected; they seemed unusually calm. Artie was puzzled. *Well,* he thought, *per- haps he had gotten there just in time—before Panther had a chance to attack.* Then something caught his eye. Over in the far corner he found three newborn kittens. Panther had chosen the coop as the safest place to deliver her litter.

Now, Artie was in a quandary. Should he move the kittens? She hadn't touched his birds, but would she in the future? He decided to wait out of sight and watch what Panther did when she returned.

Sure enough, when the cat came back, she entered the coop. He listened, but heard nothing. As quietly as possible, he crept toward the coop. When he got close, he caught her by surprise. She was only nursing her kittens and gave him a frightened look. He felt the appeal in her eyes.

So Artie made a deal with Panther. She could stay there, and he would even feed her while she was nursing, but under no circumstances was she ever to touch his birds, not now or anytime in the future. A breach of contract would not be tolerated. Somehow, it seemed as if she understood and accepted his offer.

The birds did not like the idea at first. They fluttered a little uncomfortably whenever Panther entered the coop. However, in time, they got used to the new living arrangement.

Then, on one particularly cold and nasty day, Artie walked over to the coop and looked in. Incredulous, he blinked his eyes to make sure that the scene in front of him was real. Panther wasn't there. Instead, one of the pigeons was actually sitting on the kittens to keep them warm.

Motherhood didn't calm Panther down. After the kittens were weaned and gone, she continued to terrorize the neighborhood, with one exception: She purred for Artie, and never, ever touched his pigeons.

~Barbara Vitale

Trash-Pickin' Kitty

When I adopted a kitten from a local animal shelter, I knew I was in for a real test of my patience. I had raised two other cats, big boys now, and felt sure I was ready for the chaos a new kitten would bring back into my life—and my heart. I did all the right things, like buying top-brand, expensive cat food; a big, soft bed and all the best cat toys available. But I soon began to notice that this playful and demanding little being named Lucy had her own ideas of what was best for her.

She only wanted table scraps, she would rather sleep on *my* bed than hers and she scoffed at her store-bought toys, preferring to amuse herself for hours by stealing balls of paper out of my office wastepaper basket. As a writer, I often tried to discourage her from bothering me when I was in my office working, but, try as I might, she would sneak in and overturn the trash can, running off with a mouthful of my old notes and tossed-off ideas. I would yell at her, scold her, try to encourage her to play with her "real" toys—the ones that cost me an arm and a leg—but I could not change her. My patience was wearing thin.

Determined to turn her into a good little kitten, I started locking Lucy out of the office when I was working, only to find her sitting outside the door with big, sad eyes when I came out for a breather. Sometimes, she would dart in between my feet and go straight for the trash can before I even knew what was happening. Then I'd raise my voice and lightly tap her rump, causing her to drop the wad of paper in her mouth and slink off into a corner. I hated to scold her, but she had to stop!

The tables were about to be turned.

Not long thereafter, I realized I had accidentally thrown away a great and very timely story idea, along with a magazine editor's name and contact number, given to me by a supportive writer friend. Frantically, I searched through my half-full trash can, only to realize I had emptied it—and the story idea—the day before in time for the trash pickup. Defeated, I struggled to remember what I could of the idea that I had fleshed out, and figured I could always call my friend— until I realized she was in Europe for two weeks on vacation! I doubted she had the magazine editor's name and phone number with her on her travels.

Resigned to the fact that I would lose the lead completely—or get the info I needed only after someone else had probably covered the story—I resolved never to write ideas on scraps of paper again. Instead, I would type and save them on my computer immediately.

I sat there thinking about all the other ideas and notes I had probably tossed out prematurely or accidentally when I heard a sniffing, rooting sound and turned to find Lucy pulling out a wad of paper from my trash can. I went ballistic, chasing her out of the room and up the stairs to her little cozy corner, where I noticed a handful of other balls of paper on the floor. She hid under a chair and watched me as I picked up the scraps, swearing under my breath. But then I stopped dead—as I noticed one particular paper ball with my handwriting on it. As I unfolded it, I shook my head in disbelief! It was my story idea, and the magazine editor's name and number!

I grabbed Lucy out from under the chair and hugged her tight, smooching her and praising her. She looked at me in total shock, then snuggled her little kitten nose into my chest. I hoped that meant she forgave all my impatience and rude behavior. For, in that instant, I knew that a trash-pickin' kitten is the best kitten a writer could ever have.

No more would I try to change her or scold her for being herself. I love Lucy—just the way she is.

~Marie D. Jones

Meet Our Contributors

M.L. Charendoff lives in Elkins Park, Pennsylvania, with her husband, four kids, one dog, and her two ancient cats Morris and Chloe. An at-home mom and freelance writer, Meg is currently working on a novel and a collection of essays. Please e-mail her at *MLCharendoff@comcast.net*.

Susan Isaac received her Master of Arts in English from East Tennessee State University. She teaches Composition, American Literature, and Creative Writing at Georgia Military College. Susan enjoys reading, listening to music and writing. She completed her first mystery novel and hopes to publish it. Please e-mail her at *sisaac@gmc.cc.ga.us*.

Marie D. Jones is an ordained New Thought minister and author of *Looking for God in All the Wrong Places,* as well as over three dozen inspirational books, essays and magazine articles. She lives in San Marcos, California, with her husband, toddler son and two crazy cats.

Nancy Kucik is a copywriter for a home health and hospice agency in Birmingham, Alabama, and also does freelance writing. She enjoys reading, traveling, aerobics and volunteering with her therapy cat. Nancy and her husband currently share their home with two cats and two dogs. Email her at *nancykucik@yahoo.com.*

Joanne Liu is a writer and attorney who lives with her husband and cat in Austin, Texas. She is currently working on a young adult novel about cats. Please e-mail her at *jliutex@yahoo.com.*

Roberta Lockwood received her Master's Degree in Counseling from Washington State University in 1978. She is a life coach, specializing in personal environmental design and creative expression. She enjoys writing, painting, traveling, knitting, quilting, handmade books, animals, nature and gardening. E-mail her at *robertalockwood@hotmail.com*.

Janet Mullen is Director of the Cat and Kitten Adoption Program at Noah's Ark Animal Foundation (www.noahsark.org). She enjoys traveling, reading and grandparenting. Please e-mail her at *cats@noahsark.org*.

Sheila Sowder began writing fiction after retiring from an advertising career in Washington, D.C., and Indianapolis. She was awarded the 2002 Rose Voci Fellowship for Women Writers, has had several stories and essays published in literary journals, and is currently writing a mystery. Please e-mail her at *sksowder@aol.com*.

Carol Steiner received her Bachelor of Music and Master of Music degrees from Bowling Green State University in 1967 and 1971. She taught elementary, middle school and high school music for eighteen years. She enjoys swimming, exercise, playing piano, and working with children and animals. She and her husband Ray are active in Michigan Siamese Rescue.

Hoyt Tarola is retired from the daily rigors of the business world. He spends his winters on the coast in California surfing his favorite point breaks and his summers fly-fishing in southwestern Montana. His cat, Moki, is with him wherever he goes.

Barbara Vitale, retired after more than thirty-three years as a physical educator, now continues to work as a personal trainer specializing in water therapy and water aerobics, and substitute teaches in schools. She is the author of *An Amazing Woman, the Helene Hines Story,*

Living with MS and Enjoying Life, coauthor of *Physical Education Planners,* and several short stories.

Meet Our Authors

Jack Canfield is the co-creator of the *Chicken Soup for the Soul* series, which *Time* magazine has called "the publishing phenomenon of the decade." Jack is also the coauthor of many other bestselling books.

Jack is the CEO of the Canfield Training Group in Santa Barbara, California, and founder of the Foundation for Self-Esteem in Culver City, California. He has conducted intensive personal and professional development seminars on the principles of success for more than a million people in twenty-three countries, has spoken to hundreds of thousands of people at more than 1,000 corporations, universities, professional conferences and conventions, and has been seen by millions more on national television shows.

Jack has received many awards and honors,

including three honorary doctorates and a Guinness World Records Certificate for having seven books from the *Chicken Soup for the Soul* series appearing on the *New York Times* bestseller list on May 24, 1998.

You can reach Jack at
www.jackcanfield.com.

Mark Victor Hansen is the co-founder of Chicken Soup for the Soul, along with Jack Canfield. He is a sought-after keynote speaker, bestselling author, and marketing maven. Mark's powerful messages of possibility, opportunity, and action have created powerful change in thousands of organizations and millions of individuals worldwide.

Mark is a prolific writer with many bestselling books in addition to the *Chicken Soup for the Soul* series. Mark has had a profound influence in the field of human potential through his library of audios, videos, and articles in the areas of big thinking, sales achievement, wealth building, publishing success, and personal and professional development. He is also the founder of the MEGA Seminar Series.

Mark has received numerous awards that honor his entrepreneurial spirit, philanthropic heart, and business acumen. He is a lifetime member of the Horatio Alger Association of Distinguished Americans.

You can reach Mark at
www.markvictorhansen.com.

What Jacques Cousteau did for the oceans, what Carl Sagan did for space, **Dr. Marty Becker** is doing for pets.

As a veterinarian, author, university educator, media personality and pet lover, Dr. Becker is one of the most widely recognized animal health authorities in the world. He is also passionate about his work, fostering the affection-connection between pets and people that we call, "The Bond."

Marty coauthored *Chicken Soup for the Pet Lover's Soul, Chicken Soup for the Cat & Dog Lover's Soul, Chicken Soup for the Horse Lover's Soul* and *The Healing Power of Pets,* which was awarded a prestigious silver award in the National Health Information Awards.

Dr. Becker has powerful media platforms, including seven years as the popular veterinary contributor to ABC-TV's *Good Morning America*. Dr. Becker authors two highly regarded newspaper columns that are internationally distributed by Knight Ridder Tribune (KRT) Services. And in association with the American Animal Hospital Association (AAHA), Dr. Becker hosts a nationally syndicated radio program, *Top Vet Talk Pets* on the Health Radio Network.

Dr. Becker has been featured on *ABC, NBC, CBS, CNN, PBS, Unsolved Mysteries* and in *USA Today, The New York Times, The Washington Post, Reader's Digest, Forbes, Better Homes & Gardens, The Christian Science Monitor, Woman's Day, National Geographic Traveler, Cosmopolitan, Glamour, Parents* and major Web sites such as *ABCNews.com, Amazon.com, Prevention.com, Forbes.com* and *iVillage.com*.

The recipient of many awards, Dr. Becker holds one especially dear. In 2002, the Delta Society and the American Veterinary Medical Association (AVMA) presented Dr. Becker with the prestigious Bustad Award, as the Companion Animal Veterinarian of the Year for the United States.

Marty and his family enjoy life in northern Idaho and share Almost Heaven Ranch with two dogs, five cats and five quarter horses.

Contact Marty Becker at:

P.O. Box 2775

Twin Falls, ID 83303

Phone: 208-734-8174

Web site: *www.drmartybecker.com*

Carol Kline is passionate about cats! In addition to being a doting "pet parent," she is active in animal rescue work. Although she has recently relocated to California, she is still a member of the board of directors of the Noah's Ark Animal Foundation, *www.noahsark.org,* located in Fairfield, Iowa, a limited-access, "cageless," no-kill shelter that rescues lost, stray and abandoned dogs and cats. For the last eight years, Carol has spent many hours a week monitoring the fate of dogs and cats at Noah's Ark and working to find them good permanent homes. She also administered the Caring Community Spay/Neuter Assistance Program (CCSNAP), a fund especially designated for financially assisting pet owners to spay and neuter their pets. "The reward of helping these animals is more fulfilling than any paycheck I could ever receive.

Volunteering time with the animals fills my heart and brings great joy to my life."

A freelance writer/editor for nineteen years, Carol, who has a B.A. in literature, has written for newspapers, newsletters and other publications. In addition to her own *Chicken Soup* books, she has also contributed stories and her editing talents to many other books in the *Chicken Soup for the Soul* series.

In addition to her writing and animal work, Carol is a motivational speaker and gives presentations to animal-welfare groups around the country on a variety of topics. She has also taught stress-management techniques to the general public since 1975.

Carol has the good fortune to be married to Larry and is a proud stepmother to Lorin, twenty-three, and McKenna, twenty. She has three dogs—all rescues—Beau, Beethoven and Jimmy.

To contact Carol, write to her at:
P.O. Box 521
Ojai, CA 93024
E-mail: *ckline@lisco.com*

Amy D. Shojai is an animal behavior consultant, award-winning author, lecturer, and a nationally known authority on pet care and behavior. She is a passionate proponent of owner education in her books, articles, columns and media appearances, and has been recognized by her peers as "one of the most authoritative and thorough pet reporters."

The former veterinary technician has been a full-time pet journalist for more than two decades. She is a member of the International Association of Animal Behavior Consultants and consults with a wide range of animal care professionals, researchers and other experts, and specializes in translating "medicalese" into easily understood jargon- free language to make it accessible to all pet lovers. Amy answers pet questions in her weekly "Emotional Health" column at *www.catchow.com*, hosts "Your Pet's Well-Being with Amy Shojai" at *iVillage.com* and is section leader for the Holistic and Behavior/Care portions of the PetsForum. She is also the author of twenty-one nonfiction pet books, including *PETiquette: Solving Behavior Problems in Your Multipet House-*

hold and *Complete Care for Your Aging Dog,* and a coauthor of *Chicken Soup for the Cat Lover's Soul.*

In addition to writing and pet care consulting, Amy's performance background (B.A. in music and theater) aids in her media work as a corporate spokesperson and pet product consultant. She has appeared on *Petsburgh USA/Disney* Channel Animal Planet series, *Good Day New York, Fox News: Pet News, NBC Today Show* and made hundreds of radio appearances including *Animal Planet Radio.* Amy has been featured in *USA Weekend, The New York Times, The Washington Post, Reader's Digest, Woman's Day, Family Circle, Woman's World,* as well as the "pet press." As a founder and president emeritus of the Cat Writers' Association, a member of the Dog Writers Association of America and the Association of Pet Dog Trainers, her work has been honored with over two dozen writing awards from these and many other organizations.

Amy and her husband, Mahmoud, live among 700-plus antique roses and assorted critters at Rosemont, their thirteen-acre "spread" in north Texas.

To contact Amy, write to her at:
P.O. Box 1904
Sherman, TX 75091
E-mail: *amy@shojai.com*
Web site: *www.shojai.com*

Chicken Soup for the Soul
Improving Your Life Every Day

Real people sharing real stories—for twenty years. Now, Chicken Soup for the Soul has gone beyond the bookstore to become a world leader in life improvement. Through books, movies, DVDs, online resources and other partnerships, we bring hope, courage, inspiration and love to hundreds of millions of people around the world. Chicken Soup for the Soul's writers and readers belong to a one-of-a-kind global community, sharing advice, support, guidance, comfort, and knowledge.

Chicken Soup for the Soul stories have been translated into more than forty languages and can be found in more than one hundred countries. Every day, millions of people experience a Chicken Soup for the Soul story in a book, magazine, newspaper or online. As we share our life experiences through these stories, we offer hope, comfort and inspiration to one another. The stories travel from person to person, and from country to country, helping to improve lives everywhere.

Share with Us

We all have had Chicken Soup for the Soul moments in our lives. If you would like to share your story or poem with millions of people around the world, go to chickensoup.com and click on "Submit Your Story." You may be able to help another reader, and become a published author at the same time. Some of our past contributors have launched writing and speaking careers from the publication of their stories in our books!

Our submission volume has been increasing steadily—the quality and quantity of your submissions has been fabulous. We only accept story submissions via our website. They are no longer accepted via mail or fax.

To contact us regarding other matters, please e-mail webmaster@chickensoupforthesoul.com, or fax or write us at:

Chicken Soup for the Soul
P.O. Box 700
Cos Cob, CT 06807-0700
Fax: 203-861-7194

One more note from your friends at Chicken
Soup for the Soul: Occasionally, we receive an
unsolicited book manuscript from one of our readers, and we would like to respectfully inform you
that we do not accept unsolicited manuscripts and
we must discard the ones that appear.